THE LORD'S PRAYER

LAPRIYÈ SENYÈ A

Written by
Berwick Augustin

Printed in the United States of America

Designed and illustrated by James Christy Bazile

Translated by Evoke180

ISBN-13- 978-1733076715

Our Father in heaven.

Papa nou ki nan syèl la.

1

Discussion Question

1-What does it mean to have a "FATHER in heaven"?

-Kisa sa vle di lè w gen yon "PAPA nan syèl la"?

Hallowed be your name.

Nou mande pou yo toujou respekte non ou.

Discussion Question

2-What does it mean to honor God? What has he done to deserve our praise?

-Kisa sa vle di lè w onore Bondye? Kisa li fè pou merite lwanj nou?

Your kingdom come.

Vin etabli gouvènman ou.

5

Discussion Question

3- Why is God's kingdom better for everyone?

-Poukisa wayòm Bondye a pi bon pou tout moun?

Your will be done on earth as it is in heaven.

Pou yo fè volonte ou sou latè, tankou
nan syèl la.

Discussion Question

4-How can God help me understand what I should do and how I should do it?

-Kijan Bondye ka ede mwen konprann sa mwen ta dwe fè ak kijan mwen ta dwe fè sa?

Give us this day our daily bread.
Manje nou bezwen an, ban nou li jodi a.

Discussion Question

5-How does God provide for my needs and the needs of my family, friends, church, and community?

-Kijan Bondye fè pwovizyon pou bezwen mwen yo ak bezwen fanmi mwen, zanmi mwen, legliz mwen, ak kominote mwen?

Forgive our sins.

Padonnen tout sa nou fè ki mal

11

Discussion Question

6-Why is it important for God to forgive you?

-Poukisa li enpòtan pou Bondye padone ou?

As we forgive those who sin against us.
Menm jan nou padonnen moun ki fè nou mal.

Discussion Question

7-Why is it important for you to forgive others?

-Poukisa li enpòtan pou ou padone lòt moun?

Pa kite nou pran nan pyèj.

15

Discussion Question

How can God help you do the right thing even when it's hard?

-Kijan Bondye ka ede w fè sa ki byen menm lè li difisil?

But deliver us
from the evil one.

Men, delivre nou anba dyab la.

Discussion Question

9-Why is it important to ask God to protect you from evil at all times?

-Poukisa li enpòtan pou mande Bondye pou pwoteje nou kont sa ki mal toutan?

For the kingdom, the power, and the glory are yours.

Paske tout otorite, tout pouvwa, ak tout lwanj se pou ou.

Discussion Question

10-What are the different ways we can praise God?

-Ki diferan fason nou ka bay Bondye lwanj?

Now and forevermore. Amen.

Depi koulye a ak pou tout tan. Amèn.

Discussion Question

11-What does "forever" look like?

-Kisa "pou tout tan" reyèlman vle di?

1803-THE HAITIAN FLAG

The Haitian Flag is a story of two elementary aged kids who are eager to participate in an annual Haitian Flag Day celebration at their school. They come to appreciate their culture after their parents teach them about the history, meaning, and symbolism of the Haitian flag.

Children's Historical Fiction/
978-0-9991822-1-5

1803-BLACK FREEDOM

1803-Black Freedom is the second book in a series of bilingual stories that promote Haiti's culture and history. The plot is centered around Pouchon, a middle school student of Haitian descent, who is trying out for his school's soccer team. His short stature makes him believe it's impossible to compete and make the team against bigger and faster classmates. Upon learning about Haiti's impossible victory over France in 1803 to liberate the island and blacks across the world, Pouchon is ready to use the motivation from Bataille de Vertiteres to fulfill his soccer dreams.

Children's Historical Fiction/
978-1795490771

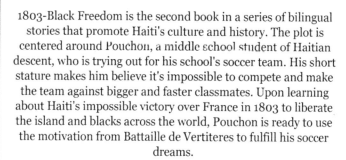

1803 SERIES WORKBOOKS (Student & Teacher's Editions)

The 1803 workbooks are designed to help young learners from K-12 practice the skills that are demanded of today's standards. Students will draw, write, create, and apply developmentally appropriate reading skills while using text-based evidence to answer questions.

ALSO BY BERWICK AUGUSTIN

NUMBERED WORDS

Words are powerful! They can either breathe or suffocate life. Many times wordiness can defeat the effectiveness of a message. This book is designed to convey succinct poems packed with powerful lessons. The poem's numerical number determines the amount of words it contains; the first one has 1 word while the fiftieth poem has 50 words.

Poetry/978-0999182208

EVOKE180 LLC Publishing   www.evoke180.com

Made in the USA
Middletown, DE
05 April 2025

73751031R00015